A

W9-BJC-791

ABORTION

INTERPRETING THE CONSTITUTION

— CAROL HAND —

PUBLISHING®

New York

Published in 2015 by The Rosen Publishing Group, Inc.
29 East 21st Street, New York, NY 10010

Copyright © 2015 by The Rosen Publishing Group, Inc.

First Edition

Library of Congress Cataloging-in-Publication Data

Hand, Carol, 1945– author.
Abortion: interpreting the Constitution/Carol Hand.
    pages cm—(Understanding the United States
    Constitution)
Includes bibliographical references and index.
ISBN 978-1-4777-7510-3 (library bound)
1. Abortion—Law and legislation—United States—Juvenile
literature. 2. Constitutional law—United States—Juvenile
literature. I. Title.
KF3771.H36 2014
342.7308'4—dc23

                                        2013041607

Manufactured in China

INTRODUCTION

Texas state senator Wendy Davis, seen here in July 2013, made national news when she filibustered the Texas Senate's highly restrictive abortion bill in June 2013.

I t was Tuesday, June 26, 2013. The Texas Senate was in the final day of a thirty-day special session when Senator Wendy Davis began a filibuster that was to last nearly eleven hours. She spoke nonstop against a bill that would close thirty-seven of the state's forty-two abortion clinics and otherwise greatly restrict abortion in the state. Republicans strongly supported the bill, and Democrats (including Davis) strongly opposed it. In the Republican Senate, the bill was expected to pass easily. But Davis, with the backing of Senate Democrats and women across the state, hoped to delay (and if possible, prevent) the vote.

While she was speaking—as long as she stayed on topic—the Senate could not vote. During the filibuster, Davis had to go without food, water, and bathroom breaks. Senate rules did not permit her to sit down or to lean on anything for support. As Davis's filibuster progressed, people around the state and country began to take notice. The area within and outside the Senate chamber filled with both supporters and protesters. Davis's Twitter following increased from 1,200 on Tuesday morning to more than 20,000 by Tuesday night. Approximately 180,000 people watched the filibuster live online.

Finally, about ten minutes before midnight, the Republican majority forced a vote to end Davis's filibuster. More than four hundred supporters in the Senate chamber shouted and chanted until midnight to prevent the vote. When a vote was finally taken, the measure passed 19–10. But the vote occurred after midnight (when the special session ended), so it was invalidated. Davis and her supporters had won—for the moment. Texas lieutenant governor David Dewhurst called the demonstrators who helped prevent the vote "an unruly mob." Senator Juan

Hinohosa, a Democrat, said, "This is democracy. They have a right to speak."

Texas governor Rick Perry, a Republican who strongly favored the bill, immediately called a second special session. On July 13, the bill passed by a vote of 19–11. During this session as well, thousands of supporters and protestors mobbed the Capitol and tried to testify. As the vote was cast, protesters outside the Senate chamber shouted "Shame! Shame!" Governor Perry called the bill Texas's "final step in our historic effort to protect life."

The Texas antiabortion bill is one of the strictest in the country. It bans abortions after twenty weeks of pregnancy; requires doctors to have admitting privileges at hospitals within 30 miles (48 kilometers), which is difficult in highly rural Texas; and requires clinics to meet the same standards as hospital-style surgical centers (renovations are too expensive for most clinics). Texas is one of many states currently enacting highly restrictive abortion laws, in spite of several U.S. Supreme Court decisions affirming women's right to abortion. A fight many thought they had won with the Supreme Court's 1973 *Roe v. Wade* decision had boiled over—this time in state legislatures.

CHAPTER ONE

LIFE BEFORE ABORTION RIGHTS

For many years, the issue of abortion has divided people into two strongly opposed groups. Those favoring abortion rights (the pro-choice group) feel that women should be free to make these personal and medical decisions with the help of their doctors. The antiabortion (pro-life) group frames the issue as a moral decision and defines abortion as murder. This division differs from the historical view of abortion in America. Both sides will be discussed here. First, a little history.

Pro-life and pro-choice advocates come face-to-face in a Washington, D.C., demonstration on January 23, 2006, as thousands of demonstrators mark the thirty-third anniversary of *Roe v. Wade*.

ABORTION AS A MEDICAL PROCEDURE

When the U.S. Constitution was adopted in 1787, abortion before quickening was not only legal, it was taken for granted. Abortion was treated as any other medical procedure; remedies were advertised openly. Usually the procedure involved taking herbs. Later, commercial remedies (some poisonous and even fatal) became available. The first laws regulating abortion, in the 1820s and 1830s, banned these poisonous abortifacients, but not abortion itself.

The field of women's reproductive services changed in the mid-1800s, when university training became required for physicians. Previously there were few restrictions on who could practice medicine. Midwives, homeopaths, and other "irregulars" (quacks and people without university training) provided most contraception, abortion, and childbirth services. With the formation of the American Medical Association (AMA) in 1841, physicians realized that restricting reproductive services to physicians only would give them financial and social benefits. The doctors pressed for legislation to outlaw irregulars from performing these services. They joined forces with a new political party, the Know-Nothings, whose beliefs combined anti-immigration (then called "nativism") and religious bigotry. In those days, the typical abortion patient was a married middle- or upper-class white Protestant woman. Because few other methods of birth control were available, the Know-Nothings suspected that Protestant women were using abortion as a form of birth control and therefore sought to criminalize it. Know-Nothings feared they would lose political control if the flood of new immigrants, particularly Irish Catholics, out-reproduced the "native" white Anglo-Saxon Protestants.

ABORTION AS A CRIMINAL ACT

In the late 1800s, individual states began to ban abortion. By 1910, men in medicine and politics had succeeded in criminalizing abortion in all but one state. Abortion was legal only when a physician decided it was necessary to save a woman's life. Doctors painted abortion as immoral and dangerous. Some women also joined the movement. Most of them supported "social purity" campaigns to restrict pursuits they considered immoral, including gambling, drinking, prostitution, and sex for purposes other than procreation.

Legally banning abortions did not prevent them. An estimated two million abortions were performed

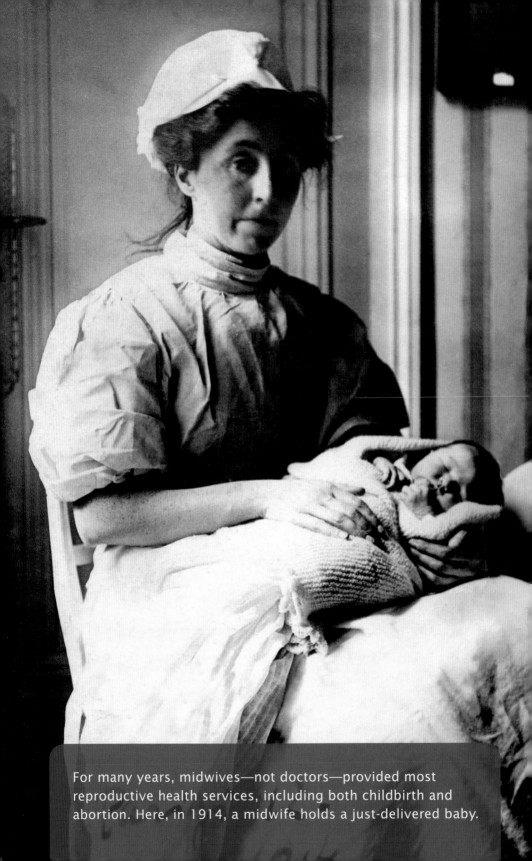

For many years, midwives—not doctors—provided most reproductive health services, including both childbirth and abortion. Here, in 1914, a midwife holds a just-delivered baby.

annually during this time (about seven to eight times more per capita than occur today). Doctors and mid-wives continued to practice the procedure with few repercussions. Historian Leslie J. Reagan feels the main effect of criminalizing abortion was to expose and humiliate women, thereby helping maintain the strict gender roles of the time.

THE COMSTOCK LAW

At around this time, Anthony Comstock, head of the New York Society for the Suppression of Vice (NYSSV), put his stamp on U.S. abortion laws by championing an act that has lasted more than a century. A devout Christian, Comstock fought against "obscenity," which he defined as including pornography, prostitution, and contraception. In 1873, Congress passed an antiobscenity bill that Comstock wrote. The Comstock Law of 1873 made it illegal to sell or distribute any materials that could be used for contraception or abortion, to send such materials (or information about them) through the U.S. mail, or to import them from abroad. For the next forty-two years, Comstock enforced his own law as a special agent for the U.S. Postal Service. By the early 1900s, twenty-four states had enacted their own versions of the Comstock Law. Some were even stricter than

Margaret Sanger (1883–1966), shown here in 1917, was trained as a nurse. She coined the term "birth control" and worked her entire adult life for women's reproductive rights.

Comstock's federal version.

The first challenge to the Comstock Law came from birth control advocate Margaret Sanger. In 1916, Sanger served thirty days in jail for opening the country's first birth control clinic. Two years later, the New York Court of Appeals' decision by Judge Frederick Crane legalized the use of birth control for "therapeutic purposes" within the state of New York. In 1936, a U.S. Circuit Court of Appeals case, *United States v. One Package*, allowed doctors to distribute contraceptives across state lines. This opened the way for legalizing birth control. In the case of *Griswold v. Connecticut* (1965), the Supreme Court ruled that restricting access to birth control was unconstitutional because it interfered with a person's right to privacy. In 1983, the Supreme Court (*Bolger v. Youngs Drug Products Corp.*) removed the final restriction of the Comstock act on contraceptive information. This decision defines contraceptive advertisements as commercial speech and protects sending them through the mail.

However, in the twenty-first century, the Comstock Law is still on the books. The last references to contraception were deleted in 1983, but—despite the Supreme Court's 1973 *Roe v. Wade* decision—the restrictions of the Comstock Law on abortion-related information still stand and have twice been strengthened. In 1994, Congress increased the fine for first-time violation of the Comstock Law from $5,000 to $250,000. In 1996, the act was amended again, making it illegal to send abortion-related information over the Internet, as well as through the mail.

PUBLIC VS. PRIVATE

During the century when abortion was illegal in the United States, people typically divided society into a "public sphere" composed of business and politics and controlled by men, and a "private sphere" or domestic world inhabited by women and children. This view ignored working-class women, women of color, and women's influence in business and politics. Early laws banning abortion were shaped by men—primarily doctors and politicians. (It should be noted that this male coalition also enabled the relaxation of abortion laws nearly a century later.) Where the "public" and "private" spheres overlapped—two distinct areas related to reproductive health care—were the home and the doctor's office.

During the Depression years of the 1930s, there were few effective contraceptive methods. Condoms and herbal remedies were popular. More effective methods, such as the use of a diaphragm, required a doctor visit, which was expensive and embarrassing for some women. Many women relied on over-the-counter chemicals advertised as "feminine hygiene" products. These often did not work, and some were dangerous. Between 1930 and 1960, the most common product used for "feminine hygiene" was Lysol disinfectant. Many people were out of work, and social safety nets to help struggling families were limited or nonexistent.

Condoms were one of the earliest birth control methods, but they were not always reliable. Here, a 1930s laboratory in the United Kingdom tests condoms.

Consider what might happen when a woman acci-
dentally became pregnant during this period of time.
Contraception has failed and the wife fears having an
illegal abortion, but the family cannot afford another

THE CASE OF
DR. JANE HODGSON

In 1970, Dr. Jane Hodgson, an obstetrician/gynecolo-
gist from Minneapolis, Minnesota, performed an
abortion on a twenty-three-year-old patient who was
exposed to German measles early in pregnancy. The
baby could have had serious physical or mental
defects, but the abortion was illegal because
Minnesota law allowed abortion only to save the
mother's life. Dr. Hodgson was tried, convicted, and
sentenced to thirty days in jail and one year proba-
tion. *Roe v. Wade* was decided before completion of
her appeal. Dr. Hodgson stated, "As doctors, we all
tend to be rigid and moralistic. Instead, we should
strive to be more humanistic, more involved with the
needs of society and individual patient.... A doctor
must always be able to choose the proper course for
the patient, or to guide the patient to make the
choice. A competent physician—not a legislator—is
in the best position to decide." Though Dr. Hodgson's
sentence was eventually suspended, she continued
championing abortion rights.

child. Desperate, the wife explains the situation to her doctor. The doctor hears tales such as this not from just one patient, but from many. He is sympathetic; his patients may even be friends. But the AMA and state laws forbid him from performing an abortion unless the patient has been raped or the pregnancy endangers her life. If he defies the law, he could lose his license and be jailed. If the woman finds an illegal abortionist and turns up injured at an emergency room, the hospital must report her to the authorities.

During the 1940s and 1950s, abortion moved from homes and private doctors' offices into hospitals and clinics, where it was much more visible. This made laws easier to enforce, and those in power enforced them with a vengeance. They hoped to repress the upwelling of feminists who were beginning to demand rights not only over their own bodies, but also in the workplace and in politics.

THE ABORTION UNDERGROUND

As antiabortion laws were more strictly enforced, a double standard quickly developed. Rich white women could afford and obtain abortions; poor or non-white women could not. Women who lacked access to safe abortions sought out untrained practitioners or attempted self-abortion, often under

BACK-ALLEY ABORTION

Dr. Waldo Fielding did his gynecological training in New York City from 1948 to 1953, where he saw firsthand the complications of illegal abortions. Sometimes, a coat hanger—that classic symbol of back-alley abortions—was still in place when a

As antiabortion fervor heats up in the 1990s, a pro-choice demonstrator holds up a coat hanger to symbolize the dangers of returning to a society where abortion is illegal.

woman arrived at the hospital. Sometimes the implement was a darning needle, crochet hook, cut-glass salt shaker, or broken soda bottle. Lacking modern equipment such as ultrasound or CT scans, doctors simply anesthetized the patient and carefully removed the implement, hoping it had not punctured the abdominal cavity. In the worst case that Dr. Fielding saw, a nurse arrived with part of her intestine hanging out. Doctors did six hours of surgery to remove her infected uterus and ovaries and repair the remaining intestine. Women never told doctors who had done their abortions or why, Fielding said, but the risks they took spoke of their desperation.

primitive and unsanitary conditions. Minnesota doctor Mildred Hanson describes how she learned about this situation: "In 1935, when I was eleven years old, my mother left our Wisconsin house on a bitter February night and dashed to the farm next door to help an ailing woman who'd had an illegal abortion. Our neighbor was writhing in pain so severe that she was having convulsions and was chewing her lip raw. It took her two days to die of blood poisoning. She left six children behind—and left me with firsthand knowledge of the injustice of illegal abortion."

Many women came to hospital emergency rooms, and some died from botched abortions. Concern over the growing danger from illegal abortions led some private doctors to defy the law. But this practice began to decline as enforcement became more rigid. An abortion "underground" developed, in which members of the feminist movement directed women to locations where they could receive safe abortions. Some members of a Chicago group called Jane even learned to perform abortions themselves. Jane helped pregnant women of all ages, races, ethnicities, and social classes.

A CHANGE IN ATTITUDE

The main impetus for relaxing state abortion laws came from two male-dominated professional organizations. The first was the medical profession that, a century before, had campaigned to criminalize abortion. A few physicians began to challenge antiabortion laws, as they saw the toll they were taking on women's lives and health. The second group was the

American Law Institute, composed of judges and law-yers. They developed a "model law" calling for legalization of abortions in cases of rape, incest, fetal abnormality, and protection of the pregnant woman's life and health. Between 1967 and 1970, nineteen states passed laws of this type.

As reporter Molly M. Ginty stated, "Outlawing abortion doesn't make it go away; it just makes it less safe." This was the situation in the early 1970s, as the Supreme Court considered the case of *Roe v. Wade*.

CHAPTER TWO

ABORTION AND THE CONSTITUTION

Although the U.S. Constitution never specifically mentions abortion, judges have interpreted several individual rights to include abortion. State and federal rulings based on these individual rights form a body of work that describes how courts have interpreted the abortion issue through the years.

CONSTITUTIONAL AMENDMENTS AND INDIVIDUAL RIGHTS

The original U.S. Constitution barely mentioned individual, or personal, rights of citizens. Its authors considered these rights so obvious, they did not need to be specifically stated. Thomas Jefferson, however, disagreed, as did the Anti-Federalists, who felt the government might take away individual rights if they were not spelled out. This fear led to the Bill of Rights, or the first ten amendments to the Constitution. The Bill of Rights primarily relates to an individual's interaction with the government or with society—for example, freedom of speech or religion and right to a fair trial. Later amendments expanded rights to include other groups—for example, civil rights for all citizens and voting rights for blacks and women.

Three of the original ten amendments specifically refer to individual rights. Amendment IV states: "The right of the people to be secure in their persons, houses, papers, and effects, against unreasonable searches and seizures, shall not be violated...." Amendment V states: "No person shall...be deprived of life, liberty, or property, without

Thomas Jefferson thought the Constitution should define people's individual rights, lest these rights be lost. This concern led to the Bill of Rights, the first ten amendments to the Constitution.

due process of law...." Amendment IX states, "The enumeration in the Constitution of certain rights shall not be construed to deny or disparage others retained by the people." In addition, one section of Amendment XIV (the Civil Rights Amendment, ratified in 1868), refers to individual rights. Section 1 states, "No State

The signers of the U.S. Constitution—all men—approved the Constitution without a Bill of Rights. But even when added, it did not address personal (including reproductive) rights.

shall make or enforce any law which shall abridge the privileges or immunities of citizens of the United States; nor shall any State deprive any person of life, liberty, or property, without due process of law...." In short, the Constitution in several places appears to protect an individual's personal life and provides no

specific rules restricting an individual's personal conduct. In Amendment XIV, it further restricts individual states from making laws that restrict these rights.

We cannot definitely know what rights the Founding Fathers considered obvious. However, based on accepted colonial customs, it seems likely that abortion (along with other very personal matters) was assumed to be a right and did not need to be addressed in the Constitution or its amendments. In other words, individuals were entitled to privacy. This right to privacy forms the foundation for rulings that led to abortion rights in the twentieth century. Although *Roe v. Wade* is the best known, other rulings, both before and since, help define the issue.

GRISWOLD V. CONNECTICUT (1965)

In the 1960s, under Connecticut law, anyone dispensing birth control information or devices risked fines and/or imprisonment. The Planned Parenthood League of Connecticut gave medical advice on birth control to married couples. When executives Estelle Griswold and Dr. C. Lee Buxton were arrested and found guilty, they appealed to the U.S. Supreme Court, which ruled the Connecticut law unconstitutional. The Court ruled that the rights of privacy guaranteed in the First, Third, Fourth, and Ninth Amendments combined to form a new constitutional right, the right to privacy in marital relations, which the Connecticut law violated. This verdict ended a forty-year fight for the right to use contraception. Although the case was not specifically about abortion, it is the first case in which the Supreme Court recognized an individual's fundamental right to privacy. The ruling became a precedent for use of the privacy argument when considering a woman's right to abortion.

UNITED STATES V. VUITCH (1969)

A statute enacted under the District of Columbia Code of 1901 made abortion a felony in the district unless it was performed under the direction of a "competent licensed practitioner of medicine" and only to preserve "the mother's life or health." A person convicted of this felony could spend from one to ten years in prison. In 1969, Dr. Milan Vuitch was sued for performing abortions in the D.C. area and challenged the statute.

The federal district court separated the law into its two parts. Based on medical evidence, it ruled that, for safety reasons, Congress has the power to outlaw abortions not performed by a medical professional, making this part of the law constitutional. However, the second part, banning abortions except to preserve "the mother's life or health," was less clear. The word "health" was not defined, so there was no way to determine the degree of health required or whether it included both mental and physical health. The court's ruling stated, in part, "The jury's acceptance or

UNITED STATES V. SHIRLEY A. BOYD

Shirley A. Boyd, a nurse's aide, challenged the District of Columbia abortion law at the same time as Dr. Vuitch. She challenged the court to invalidate the entire statute for several reasons: the "life and health" phrase was vague; the statute denied equal protection to women of all economic groups; and it interfered with the constitutional right of all women to decide whether to bear a child. The court agreed with her contention of vagueness but did not rule on the other two questions. It stated that, although there had been discrimination against the poor, the state could apply the statute equally because free medical care for the poor was available. Ruling on the right to privacy, the court said, would require the court to legislate, which it cannot do. The district court therefore denied Boyd's motion.

nonacceptance of an individual doctor's interpretation of the ambivalent and uncertain word 'health' should not determine whether he stands convicted of a felony, facing ten years' imprisonment. His professional judgment made in good faith should not be challenged."

This federal court appealed to the U.S. Supreme Court, which ruled that the statute was not unconstitutionally vague. However, the Court interpreted the word "health" to include both psychological and physical well-being. The Court further ruled that the burden of proof rested with the prosecutor, not the accused person, and recommended that Congress reformulate the statute more scientifically. *United States v. Vuitch* was the first case strictly about abortion to reach the Supreme Court.

ROE V. WADE (1973)

Roe v. Wade is the case primarily associated with the legalization of abortion. The plaintiff, "Jane Roe," was a single pregnant woman whose real name was Norma McCorvey. The lawsuit challenged Texas abortion law, which made abortion criminal except to save the mother's life. Roe won her case in Texas District Court, and the defendant, Dallas County district attorney Henry Wade, appealed to the Supreme Court. The Supreme Court upheld the Texas ruling in

After *Roe v. Wade* passed in 1973, defenders of the decision, such as those shown here, were immediately confronted with antiabortion groups working for its repeal.

a 7–2 decision, with Justice Harry Blackmun writing the decision. The *Roe v. Wade* ruling established that abortion is included within an individual's right to privacy. The ruling forbids states from enacting any restrictions on abortion during the first trimester. During the second and third trimesters, they may enact laws protecting the health of the mother. During the third trimester, they may enact laws protecting the life of the fetus, but they must make an exception to protect the mother's life and health.

The ruling again defined a "zone of privacy" protected by the First, Fourth, Ninth, and Fourteenth Amendments, including marriage, contraception, and child rearing. According to "The Supreme Court—Expanding Civil Rights," the Court argued that the zone of privacy was "broad enough to

HARRY A. BLACKMUN

Justice Harry A. Blackmun, author of the *Roe v. Wade* decision, grew up in a working-class neighborhood in Minneapolis, Minnesota. Blackmun obtained degrees in mathematics and law from Harvard University. He served as an associate justice of the Supreme Court from 1970 to 1994. Blackmun's early

Justice Harry A. Blackmun framed the *Roe v. Wade* decision in terms of a doctor's right to treat patients, but his later decisions emphasized women's rights.

opinions were relatively conservative; for example, he initially supported the death penalty. Later, he became increasingly passionate about protecting the rights of the disadvantaged and oppressed. He wrote more than thirty opinions addressing racial issues. Before forming his opinion on abortion, Blackmun spent months researching the subject in the Mayo Clinic library. His support for *Roe v. Wade* led to death threats and personal attacks. Although his position isolated him from conservative members of the Court, he steadfastly defended his opinion on *Roe* and fought their attempts to weaken it.

encompass a woman's decision whether or not to terminate her pregnancy." The Court argued that prenatal life was not within the U.S. Constitution's definition of "persons." It therefore followed that, since no consensus exists on whether fetuses deserve full rights, the Texas law was unconstitutional, since it took one of many possible views on this issue.

DOE V. BOLTON (1973)

The Supreme Court decided *Doe v. Bolton* and *Roe v. Wade* at the same time and intended the two decisions to be read together. Justice Blackmun also wrote the *Bolton* decision. In this suit, the Atlanta branch of the American Civil Liberties Union and the Legal Aid Society challenged Georgia's abortion law on behalf of Sandra Bensing. Bensing was indigent, pregnant, separated from her husband, and already had three children. Georgia's restrictions allowed abortion in only three situations: serious threats to the woman's health, risk of serious birth defects, or rape. Bensing met none of these conditions, therefore, the state refused her an abortion. The law also required abortions to be performed in a hospital accredited by the Joint Commission on Accreditation of Hospitals (JCAH). Further, each abortion had to be approved by the hospital's abortion committee; and the initial physician's judgment of the need for an abortion had to be confirmed by two other physicians. Finally, only Georgia residents could receive abortions.

The district court invalidated the part of the Georgia law that limited abortions to the three situations described because it represented an infringement of the right to privacy and personal liberty. However, the court retained the rest of the law. The plaintiffs appealed to the Supreme Court. By a 7–2 decision, the Supreme Court ruled that, although a woman does not have an absolute right to an abortion, her rights are much broader than the Georgia statute allowed. The Court upheld a physician's right to determine when to perform an abortion and struck down the requirements for an abortion to be performed in a JCAH-accredited hospital and for a hospital to refuse an abortion in the first three months. It also ruled that the hospital committee review restricts the patient's rights and that requiring two other physicians to "sign off" on an abortion infringes on the physician's right to practice medicine. Finally, the Court invalidated the Georgia residency requirement, ruling that it violated the privileges and immunities clause of the Fourteenth Amendment. The *Roe v. Bolton* decision further cements the principle that the due process clause of the Fourteenth Amendment provides a right to privacy that encompasses a woman's right to terminate a pregnancy.

These are the most important court decisions affecting abortion rights through *Roe v. Wade*. But these decisions did not resolve the issue. Even at the time, they were controversial. For example, the Heritage Foundation, a conservative think tank, considers these decisions "judicial activism" because the Court essentially "creates" a right that is not specifically found in the text of the Constitution. Liberals argue that the Constitution is a living document; that

The conservative Heritage Foundation openly opposes abortion and supports policies and politicians who oppose it. One of these is Newt Gingrich, former House Speaker and Republican presidential candidate.

is, the authors intended that future generations interpret it to meet the needs of the culture at that time. For a while, the 1973 decisions legalized abortion, but recently, many states have again begun to restrict or try to ban abortion.

CHAPTER THREE

THE CASE FOR ABORTION RIGHTS: A WOMAN'S CHOICE

Arguments for liberalization of abortion laws have encompassed public health, civil rights, women's equality, and racial issues. Arguments have evolved over the years, following medical advances, legal precedents, and changes in women's place in society. But an individual's right to privacy was the only issue used by the courts as the basis for the 1973 decisions that conferred abortion rights—*Roe v. Wade* and *Doe v. Bolton*.

REFORM VS. REPEAL

Until about 1970, people pushed for reform of current abortion laws. Rather than a complete ban on abortions, reformers hoped to have laws made less strict so that exceptions could be made. Suggested exceptions would allow abortion in case of danger to the mother's life or health, rape or incest, or severe physical or mental defects in the fetus. This approach, called "therapeutic abortion," was accepted by groups from the American Medical Association to the Clergy Consultation Service on Abortion. The latter group, which began in New York and later spread to twenty-six states, consisted of ministers and rabbis who helped women secure safe abortions in states where abortion was still illegal.

Soon people began to call for repeal, rather than reform, of abortion laws. In 1969, Jimmye Kimmey, executive director of the Association for the Study of Abortion, advocated reforms that permitted physicians the right to make decisions regarding abortion and accepted abortion as a normal part of medical practice. She did not mention women's rights. Three years later, in December 1972, Kimmey wrote a memorandum suggesting the phrase "Right to Choose" as an alternative to the developing "Right to Life" movement. Here, she puts women front and center, stating, "What we are concerned with is ... the woman's right to choose—not with her right (or anyone else's right) to make a choice about whether that choice is morally licit." In June 1972, a Gallup poll showed that two-thirds of Americans felt decisions on abortion should be left up to a woman and her physician.

THE PUBLIC HEALTH ARGUMENT

The public health argument centered around dangers resulting from illegal abortions. In 1959, Mary Steichen Calderone, then medical director of Planned Parenthood, cited estimates of approximately one million illegal abortions per year. She pointed out inconsistent interpretation and enforcement of laws, including the inability of poor women to obtain abortions and the need for physicians to hide the care they were giving their patients. Calderone stressed that she was not "pro-abortion," but that society should recognize the need for abortion and strive to make it unnecessary by providing reproductive education and birth control for all women.

The 1972 Rockefeller Commission Report (Commission on Population Growth and the American Future), commissioned by then President Richard Nixon, made similar arguments. The commission stated that abortion should not be considered a substitute for birth control, but that liberalized abortion access would contribute to "the exercise of individual freedom." They pointed out (citing New York's recently liberalized abortion laws) that legalizing abortion decreased numbers of maternal and infant deaths and out-of-wedlock births in addition to decreasing illegal abortions.

CIVIL RIGHTS AND WOMEN'S EQUALITY

When U.S. author and feminist Betty Friedan founded the National Organization for Women (NOW) in 1966, its Women's Bill of Rights concentrated mostly on ending workplace discrimination; reproductive rights were listed last. But by 1969, Friedan had recognized their importance. In a speech to the First National Conference on Abortion Laws in February 1969, she stated:

Betty Friedan (1921–2006), author and women's rights activist, framed abortion rights in the context of a woman's "choice to have children."

There is no freedom, no equality, no full human dignity and personhood possible for women until we assert and demand the control over our own bodies, over our own reproductive process.

There is only one voice that needs to be heard on the question of the final decision as to whether a woman will or will not bear a child, and that is the voice of the woman herself. Her own conscience, her own conscious choice.

This conference—and Friedan's passionate words—led to the formation of a new organization: the National Association for the Repeal of Abortion Laws (NARAL). Together with NOW, NARAL caused a shift from abortion reform to abortion repeal and a reframing of the issue from one of physicians' rights to one of women's rights. Not all feminists boarded the abortion rights bandwagon, however. Some, such as Catholic author Sidney Callahan, considered the "abortion on demand" argument a betrayal of the women's movement.

NON-WHITES AND ABORTION

There is no question that abortion laws were enforced inconsistently. In New York City between 1951 and 1962, more than 92 percent of women receiving

THE REDSTOCKINGS PROTEST

In February 1969, a New York legislative committee held a hearing to consider easing the state law banning all abortions. The committee invited "experts" (fourteen men and one woman—a Catholic nun) to speak. Members of the Redstockings, a radical feminist group, disrupted the meeting. They argued that men and Catholic nuns were the people least likely to understand abortion and that the real experts were women who had had abortions. Rather than allow the women to speak, the committee moved its discussion behind closed doors. The Redstockings responded by organizing the first Abortion Speak-Out on March 21, 1969, in New York City. Several hundred people listened as twelve women testified about their own experiences with restrictive abortion laws. Speak-outs in other cities quickly followed.

hospital abortions were white; more than three-fourths of those dying from illegal abortions were women of color. Yet, people of color in the twentieth century were mistrustful of the abortion rights movement. Many saw it as a form of genocide, which they had good reason to fear. Between the 1930s and 1970s, the United States undertook a eugenics program that resulted in the sterilization of tens of thousands of blacks, Native Americans, and Puerto Ricans. By the 1960s, thirty-one states had adopted eugenics programs. Often women were sterilized without their consent and were chosen because they were poor, minority, or considered "undesirable."

Many black men saw attempts to limit childbirth by black women as "race suicide," which would weaken the race and prevent them from gaining power. But while black women opposed mandated birth control (including abortion and sterilization), they also opposed efforts to force them to have children. Shirley Chisholm, the first black woman elected to Congress, was an early leader in the abortion rights movement. At first opposed to repeal of abortion laws, Chisholm later became honorary president of NARAL. She understood the harm of illegal abortions and considered both safe, effective birth control and safe, legal abortion necessary to give black women an equal chance in the workplace and in society.

Today, the situation has changed again. Black women are now four times more likely than white women to have an abortion during their lives. Blacks have a much higher rate of unintended pregnancy, due

Shirley Chisholm (1924–2005) was the first black woman elected to Congress and the first black woman to run for president (in 1971), as well as a pioneer for women's rights.

to lack of access to health care and lower use of birth control. But fear of genocide is making a comeback. The Radiance Foundation, a Georgia-based antiabortion group, sponsors billboards that say "Black children are an endangered species." A New York group, Life Always, has a billboard that says "The most dangerous place for an African American is in the womb." The leadership of these antiabortion groups is primarily black, male, and religious.

NEW YORK LEGALIZES ABORTION

The lawsuit brought against New York's antiabortion law in 1970 cited many legal arguments later used in federal cases. The original law defined as a felony any abortion other than a

Some antiabortion groups specifically target the black community, as in this 2011 billboard in New York City.

"justifiable abortional act" (one necessary to pre-serve a woman's life). The plaintiffs successfully overturned this law, making abortion legal in New York. First, they argued that the phrase "necessary to preserve the life" presented no procedures for deter-mining "necessity" and therefore failed to meet the specificity requirement of the Fourteenth Amendment. That is, if a law is not specific enough so that a citizen knows precisely what is expected, the law can be voided for vagueness. Second, they argued that the law violates the physician's right to privacy in the doctor-patient relationship. This right is considered part of the personal freedoms guaran-teed by the Bill of Rights.

Third, they claimed the right of marital privacy, defined in the Supreme Court's *Griswold v. Connecticut* (1965) decision on use of contraceptives, arguing that abortion is a logical extension of the right to use con-traceptives. Fourth, the law interferes with a physician's personal freedom by violating the right to practice medicine according to the highest standards. Other arguments included violations of liberty without due process of law, of equal protection for rich and poor women, of First Amendment prohibitions against laws establishing a religion, and of the Eighth Amendment prohibition against cruel and unusual punishment (forcing a woman to bear an unwanted child).

LIBERTY AND EQUALITY ARGUMENTS

The Supreme Court in *Roe v. Wade* zeroed in on the due processes clauses of the Fifth and Fourteenth Amendments. Both amendments protect against loss of "life, liberty, or property" without due process of law. This constitutes the "liberty" argument. Since *Roe*

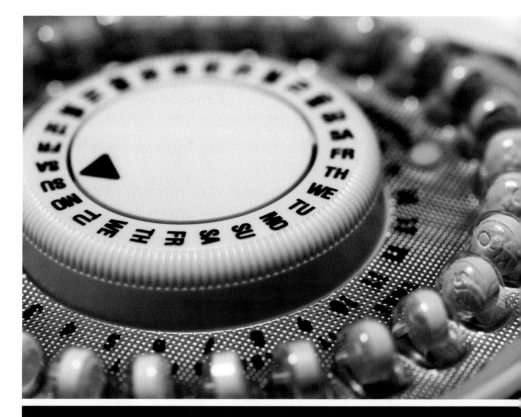

The birth control pill, approved by the U.S. Food and Drug Administration in 1960, was highly effective and gave women freedom to plan their families. It decreased birth rates, thus decreasing the need for abortions.

v. Wade, the Supreme Court has broadened this argument by affirming that the abortion right encompasses equality as well as liberty. This argument is also based on the due process clauses.

Sexual equality arguments question whether abortion restrictions are based on sex-role stereotypes. For example, do restrictions force women to give birth but provide little or no support for new mothers (placing the entire burden of support on mothers because motherhood is the "natural" role of women)? Do they prevent women from controlling the timing of motherhood, thereby increasing economic, educational, or other problems? The argument is that abortion restrictions enforcing traditional sex-role stereotypes may violate the Constitution.

In recent decisions, justices are also making equality arguments based on the equal protection clause of the Fourteenth Amendment, which states: "No State shall…deny to any person within its jurisdiction the equal protection of the laws." In *Planned Parenthood of Southeastern Pennsylvania v. Casey* (1992), a Supreme Court majority reaffirmed *Roe v. Wade* by invoking the due process clause. Justice Blackmun's separate opinion further linked the decision to the equal protection clause. Although *Casey* increased restrictions on abortion, it also upheld the notion that abortion restrictions that deny a woman's equality impose an "undue burden" on her fundamental right to decide whether to become a mother.

The equality argument is usually used to complement and strengthen the liberty argument. However, abortion rights opponents reject both arguments. They see decisions based on these clauses (including *Roe v. Wade* and *Planned Parenthood of Southeastern Pennsylvania v. Casey*) as recognizing "unenumerated rights"—that is, rights not specifically mentioned in the Constitution. (Other unenumerated rights are accepted without question, including rights to travel, marry, procreate, or use contraception—or corresponding rights not to do these things.)

The decision to have—or not to have—a child is extremely serious, and women seldom make it lightly. Birth control and abortion have made this decision possible.

People have given many justifications for abortion rights. Both social and legal arguments rely on an underlying assumption of a woman's right to liberty and equality, including her right to control her own body. Members of this side of the argument tend to view themselves not as "pro-abortion," but as "pro-choice." They advocate the woman's right to choose whether to complete or terminate a pregnancy. Choice is only possible if abortion is available under safe, medically protected conditions. Most pro-choice women do not see abortion as a preferred form of birth control. Rather, they see it as a last resort that, in a free society, must be available for use in specific situations, such as serious illness, rape, fetal abnormality, or contraceptive failure.

CHAPTER FOUR

THE CASE AGAINST ABORTION RIGHTS: THE "RIGHT TO LIFE"

A ntiabortion (right-to-life) arguments are usually moral and/or religious in nature. The basic right-to-life position is an equality argument, in which the rights of the fetus are assumed to be equal to the rights of the pregnant woman. Right-to-life supporters argue that life begins at conception, when the sperm fertilizes the egg. Thus, killing a fetus, which has the potential to become a human being, is no different than killing, say, a ten-year-old.

Molly McCann, age fifteen, marches in the fortieth annual March for Life antiabortion protest in Washington, D.C., on January 25, 2013.

CURRENT LAW AND FETAL RIGHTS

Current U.S. law does not give the fetus full rights, or "personhood," but considers it a part of the mother. However, as medical technology has advanced, it has become possible to view, diagnose, and treat the fetus as an individual patient. This has led to recent legal rulings granting limited fetal rights, which increase as the pregnancy progresses. For example, in the *Roe v. Wade* decision, an embryo or fetus has no rights during the first trimester of pregnancy. During the second trimester, aborting a fetus is legal only if maintaining the pregnancy poses significant harm to the mother. During the third trimester, the mother's life must be in danger. However, in this decision, the mother's life always takes priority. According to right-to-life advocates, this ruling translates to "abortion on demand"—that is, the mother can abort the fetus at any time during the nine months of pregnancy, if she can persuade a doctor her health or life is in danger.

Some legal scholars see an increasing need to clarify fetal rights; others fear that, in elevating fetal rights, the woman's right to control her own body will be lost or diminished. Some cases now put fetal rights in competition with maternal rights. For example, some states have begun to hold mothers

WHO WAS JANE ROE?

The young Texas woman who became "Jane Roe" was born Norma McCorvey. She dropped out of school in ninth grade and at sixteen married an abusive man. When recruited as plaintiff for *Roe v. Wade*, she was twenty-one and pregnant for the third time. She claimed she had been raped, but years later she admitted she had lied. The pro-life movement used this fact to try to discredit the *Roe* verdict. The case was decided after McCorvey gave birth; her daughter was adopted. For twenty years, McCorvey worked at women's clinics as a pro-choice advocate. But in 1995, she converted to Christianity and gave up her pro-choice beliefs. She became a pro-life activist, forming an organization called Roe No More. Both sides of the debate have exploited McCorvey at different times, but she may have changed sides too often. According to Joshua Prager of the magazine *Vanity Fair*, "McCorvey has long been less pro-choice or pro-life than pro-Norma."

Norma McCorvey *(left)* demonstrates with her lawyer, Gloria Allred, at a pro-choice rally on April 26, 1989, in front of the U.S. Supreme Court building.

criminally liable for damage to the fetus caused by prenatal drug use. In a Florida case (*Johnson v. State*, 1991), Jennifer Johnson was convicted for delivering cocaine through her umbilical cord to two of her four children. A court of appeals upheld Johnson's conviction but avoided the issue of fetal rights. The court stated that her babies had received cocaine through the umbilical cord after birth, but before the cord was cut, which constituted delivery of a controlled substance to a minor.

DEFENDING LIFE: BECKWITH'S ARGUMENT

Francis J. Beckwith, associate professor of philosophy and jurisprudence at Baylor University, Waco, Texas, a leading Baptist university, has made perhaps the most thorough analysis and defense of the pro-life argument. He outlines three premises, gives arguments supporting each premise, and having proven to his satisfaction that all three premises are true, draws a conclusion. The premises and conclusion, from his book, *Defending Life*, are as follows:

1.   "The unborn entity, from the moment of conception, is a full-fledged member of the human community.

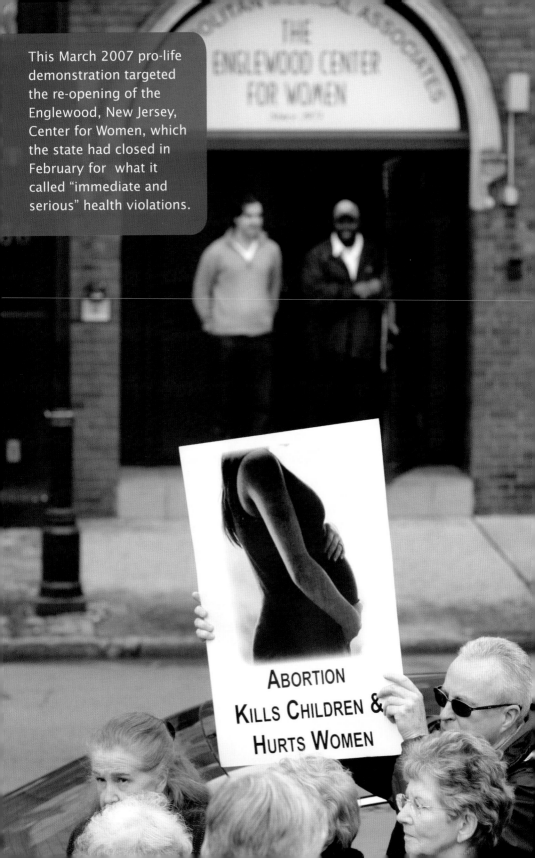

This March 2007 pro-life demonstration targeted the re-opening of the Englewood, New Jersey, Center for Women, which the state had closed in February for what it called "immediate and serious" health violations.

2. It is prima facie morally wrong to kill any member of that community.

3. Every successful abortion kills an unborn entity, a full-fledged member of the human community.

4. Therefore, every successful abortion is prima facie morally wrong."

Legally, the term "prima facie" refers to evidence that is accepted as correct until proven otherwise. As Beckwith uses it, the term suggests a statement everyone agrees with—something people generally accept as true. For example, killing a human being is generally accepted as wrong. Therefore, pro-lifers reason, if they can prove that an unborn entity (of whatever age) is a full-fledged human being, they have proven that abortion is murder.

WHEN LIFE BEGINS

If Beckwith's first premise (an unborn entity is fully human from the moment of conception) is not true, the rest of his argument is invalidated. Pro-life advocates accept this premise without question. Others have more difficulty with it. Controversies surrounding this premise fall into two camps: biological and values-driven.

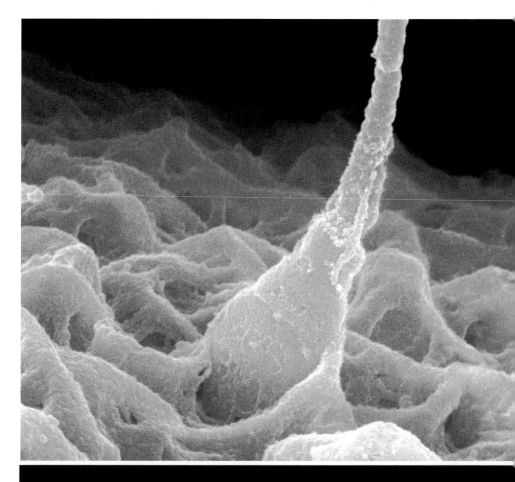

During fertilization, the sperm first penetrates the egg's outer layer; then, the genetic material of the sperm and egg merge. This is one definition of the beginning of life.

Biological arguments center around the question of when life actually begins. Many biologists define the beginning of human life as the moment of conception, or fertilization—that is, the moment when the chromosomes of egg and sperm combine to form a unique genetic entity. Unless there are medical complications (such as miscarriage), conception begins a continuous process that ultimately leads to the birth of a human baby. Other biologists feel that life begins several days later at implantation, when the embryo attaches to the uterine wall. One reason favoring the implantation argument is that a fertilized egg (zygote) can still divide to form twins. Thus, the zygote is not necessarily a unique biological entity. Only after implantation is it definitely unique.

Pro-life, values-driven arguments assume that an unborn entity is fully human from the moment of conception. Pro-choice advocates assume that full personhood does not occur until some late point in pregnancy. Usually this is the time of viability, when the unborn entity is capable of independent life outside the uterus. The timing of viability is also a matter of controversy. In 1973, when *Roe v. Wade* was decided, viability was between twenty-four and twenty-eight weeks of gestation. However, improvements in medical technology have pushed back this time. In 2013, viability was said to occur at twenty to twenty-four weeks of gestation. (In human pregnancies, full gestation is anywhere from thirty-eight to forty-two weeks.)

UNBORN EQUALITY

Pro-life advocates assume the unborn entity has equal value to a born entity, or person, from conception to birth. They feel the unborn entity has the same rights before viability that it has after viability—and after birth. According to this "substance view," a human being is intrinsically valuable because of its substance as a "rational moral agent." The human being maintains essential characteristics in spite of changes (such as growth) and retains its value throughout life, even without always exhibiting all functions of a rational moral agent. Thus, the "human substance" includes unborn entities, children, and adults with mental or physical defects as well as "normal" human beings of all ages.

However, it can be difficult to separate biological from values arguments. Within the medical profession, there are disagreements about when pregnancy itself begins. In a 2011 survey of ob-gyns (obstetrician-gynecologists), 57 percent stated that pregnancy begins at conception; 28 percent stated that it begins at implantation; and 16 percent were not sure. Answers correlated with importance of the doctor's religion and his or her beliefs about abortion—more religious doctors answered "at conception."

BECKWITH'S CONCLUSION

Beckwith's second premise, "It is prima facie morally wrong to kill any member of that community" (the human community), simply means that, under ordinary circumstances, it is morally wrong to kill another human being. He does allow for killing in extraordinary circumstances, such as self-defense or a "just war." He also allows for the possibility of killing an unborn baby, for example, if continuing the pregnancy would kill both the mother and baby. In this case, Beckwith says, the intent of an abortion is not to kill the fetus but to protect the mother's life. It is a higher good to save one life if the alternative would be the loss of both lives. This is an example of the application of pro-life principles.

In cases where the mother's life is not at stake, but she would suffer severe emotional or economic harm due to pregnancy, Beckwith and many other pro-life advocates are steadfast in their opposition to abortion. In the case of rape, the rapist, rather than the unborn entity, is considered the aggressor. Therefore, regardless of her mental health, the woman must bear the rapist's child because it is a fully human being (based on the first premise) and its life cannot be forfeited to benefit another.

Abortion ends a pregnancy, thereby terminating (killing) an embryo or fetus. Pro-life advocates strongly believe that this entity is a "full-fledged member of the human community" as soon as conception occurs. Therefore, they consider an abortion at any stage after conception to be equivalent to murder. Because everyone generally accepts that killing a human being is morally wrong, it follows logically that abortion is morally wrong.

OTHER REASONS

Most other justifications of the antiabortion viewpoint follow the premise that the unborn entity is fully human and is entitled to the same rights as "born" humans. These justifications include the ideas that civilized societies do not permit the intentional taking of a life and that the original text of the doctor's Hippocratic Oath forbids abortion. Also, followers of this viewpoint feel that abortion contradicts the intent of the Founding Fathers, stated in the Declaration of Independence, that "[A]ll men are created equal, that they are endowed by their Creator with certain unalienable rights, that among these are Life, Liberty, and the pursuit of Happiness." (This argument assumes that an unborn entity of any age is a "man.")

Some pro-life advocates propose arguments that have a dubious scientific basis or have been proven untrue. One argument, made by Dr. Kanwaljeet Anand of the University of Tennessee, is that the fetus feels pain as early as twenty weeks. According to the majority of scientific literature, although fetuses respond to touch and other stimuli by twenty weeks, the brain connections necessary to feel pain do not form until at least twenty-six weeks. A second is that having an abortion increases the risk of breast cancer in women who have been pregnant previously. This argument has been discredited by the American Cancer Society. A third is the claim that abortion leads to various psychological disorders, including depression, alcohol and drug abuse, and suicide. This claim was based on one badly designed study in which the author failed to determine whether the test subjects had the disorders before they had abortions. Finally, recent claims that a woman cannot become pregnant from rape are based on dubious mathematical calculations in a 1999 paper by former Right-to-Life president Dr. John Willke. The same (incorrect) idea is also found in medieval textbooks. Although scientifically inaccurate, these claims have been used by state and federal legislators to pass antiabortion legislation.

The major thrust of the pro-life argument is based on two factors, both of which are controversial and open to interpretation by the courts. The first of these is the question of when life begins. The pro-life movement believes life begins at conception. The second is the question of whether an unborn entity is entitled to the same rights as a born entity—that is, whether the unborn entity is "fully human" and therefore has equal standing with the born entity, or person. The pro-life movement believes that an unborn entity is fully human and thus entitled to full human rights from the moment of conception.

CHAPTER FIVE

BANNING ABORTION STATE BY STATE

T he Supreme Court decisions of *Roe v. Wade* and *Doe v. Bolton* legalized abortion, but legality did not translate to easy access for many women. The antiabortion movement vowed to stop abortions despite the Supreme Court rulings. They described these rulings as "abortion on demand." But, in fact, the rulings left considerable leeway for states to regulate times and circumstances under which women can access abortion services. In the decades since these decisions, pro-life activists have worked hard to increase restrictions at both state and federal levels. They brought lawsuits at the state level to challenge specific provisions of *Roe v. Wade*. Some of these lawsuits reached the Supreme Court.

RESTRICTIONS ON FEDERAL FUNDING

In 1977, three separate rulings (*Maher v. Roe*, *Beal v. Doe*, and *Poelker v. Doe*) upheld restrictions on public funding for abortions. In *Beal*, the Court ruled that Medicaid is only obligated to pay for "medically necessary" abortions. In *Maher*, the Court ruled that the Fourteenth Amendment's equal protection clause requires state Medicaid to cover childbirth for indigent women, but not cover nontherapeutic abortions. In *Poelker*, the Court stated that the equal protection clause does not require a public hospital to provide nontherapeutic abortions. These rulings effectively eliminated abortion as an option for many poor women.

In 1980, the Court's decision in *Harris v. McRae* upheld the Hyde Amendment, an anti-*Roe v. Wade* amendment originally passed by Congress in 1976 to limit Medicaid funding only to abortions necessary to save the mother's life. The Court stated that *Harris v. McRae* did not conflict with freedom of choice because an indigent woman is still free to choose a nontherapeutic abortion; she is just not entitled to financial help. Four justices dissented strongly, stating that this discrimination based on a person's ability to pay can "discourage the exercise of fundamental liberties just as effectively as can an outright denial of those rights...."

FURTHER WEAKENING *ROE*

Between 1996 and 1998, new Supreme Court justices made the Court much more conservative. There was no longer a clear majority of justices in favor of *Roe v. Wade*, and several cases further weakened the rulings. *Webster v. Reproductive Health Services* (1989) was the first opinion where only four justices voted to uphold *Roe* in its entirety. The decision upheld a Missouri ban on use of public facilities and employees to perform abortions, unless an abortion was necessary to save a woman's life. They also upheld the law's requirement that physicians test for viability at twenty weeks and after. Several justices urged for *Roe* to be reconsidered or even overturned. Justice Blackmun dissented, saying, "For today, the women of this Nation still retain the liberty to control their destinies. But the signs are evident and very ominous, and a chill wind blows."

Planned Parenthood of Southeastern Pennsylvania v. Casey (1992) challenged a Pennsylvania abortion law that included an informed-consent requirement, a twenty-four-hour waiting period, a requirement for minors to obtain parental consent, and a requirement for a wife to inform her husband. The case was split. Five justices upheld the validity of *Roe*. A different combination of five justices also upheld all restrictions of the Pennsylvania law except the spousal notification requirement. *Casey* was the first Supreme Court case to partially dismantle *Roe*'s trimester system. The ruling did not change restrictions after viability, but it freed states to regulate abortion before viability.

Roe v. Wade had labeled abortion a right and required state laws regulating it to be analyzed under a "strict scrutiny" standard (the most rigorous legal standard). However, Casey used the less strict "undue burden" standard. Under this standard, restrictions on abortion before viability are constitutional unless they impose an "undue burden" on the woman's right to terminate the pregnancy. Pro-life groups were dissatisfied; they had hoped Roe would be overturned. Pro-choice groups saw the decision as further weakening the right guaranteed by Roe. However, by affirming the basic Roe decision, the Court added to the legal precedent for Roe, which may make future challenges more difficult.

PARTIAL-BIRTH ABORTION LAWS

Partial-birth abortions were done in the second trimester of pregnancy, usually between twenty and twenty-four weeks, by a process known as "dilation and extraction" (D&X). In a D&X, the fetus was partially extracted from the uterus, the skull collapsed, and the body removed intact. This procedure was done rarely and only to preserve the woman's life or fertility. *Sternberg v. Carhart* (2000) challenged a Nebraska law prohibiting partial-birth abortion. The law made the D&X procedure a felony punishable by possible fines, jail time, and loss of the doctor's license. The Supreme Court ruled the law unconstitutional, based on the precedents of *Roe* and *Casey*. The Court felt the law as written was unclear because it could be interpreted to include forms of abortion other than D&X, which posed an undue burden on doctors and on women seeking abortions. Their ruling struck down similar laws in thirty states.

However, in 2003, Congress passed the Federal Partial Birth Abortion Ban Act, which banned the D&X procedure nationally. Abortion rights advocates challenged the law and lower courts struck it down, citing *Sternberg* (2000) as a precedent. The case went to the Supreme Court, and in *Gonzales v. Carhart* (2007), the Court reversed course and upheld the federal ban on the D&X procedure. This was a victory for abortion opponents.

THE STATES RISE UP

The *Gonzales v. Carhart* decision greatly emboldened antiabortion activists. The Supreme Court had weakened but not overturned *Roe v. Wade*, so activists began a coordinated state-by-state effort to elect

STATE ABORTION RESTRICTION PROVISIONS SINCE 1985

The record number of ninety-two restrictions in 2011 followed the 2010 elections, in which many governorships and legislatures became Republican-controlled. The trend continued after the 2012 election, with forty-three new restrictions enacted by mid-year 2013.

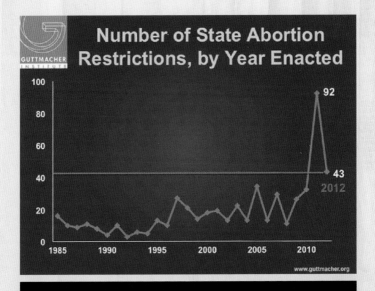

Number of State Abortion Restrictions, by Year Enacted

GUTTMACHER
INSTITUTE

92

43
2012

www.guttmacher.org

Although several Supreme Court decisions have weakened *Roe v. Wade*, none have overturned it. Pro-life groups instead turned to the states, passing more and more restrictions on abortion.

According to the Guttmacher Institute, a non-profit organization originally formed under the auspices of Planned Parenthood, almost 60 percent of women who delayed having an abortion described difficulty making arrangements and obtaining money and 58 percent would have preferred to have the procedure earlier. As of 2013, 32 percent of abortions occurred in the first six weeks of pregnancy. The trend toward very early abortions is possible, thanks to the medication abortion (Mifeprex, or "abortion pill"), which is very safe and has a 92 to 95 percent success rate. But new abortion provisions are restricting medication abortion by requiring a doctor's presence when a woman takes each pill. She cannot take the pill at home or receive care or counseling via telemedicine. Many women in Alaska and in rural areas of the West and Midwest are highly dependent on telemedicine. Studies show that results for telemedicine patients are comparable to those having face-to-face doctor visits. Yet new restrictions on medication abortion require multiple doctor visits, increasing cost, time, and transportation requirements for women.

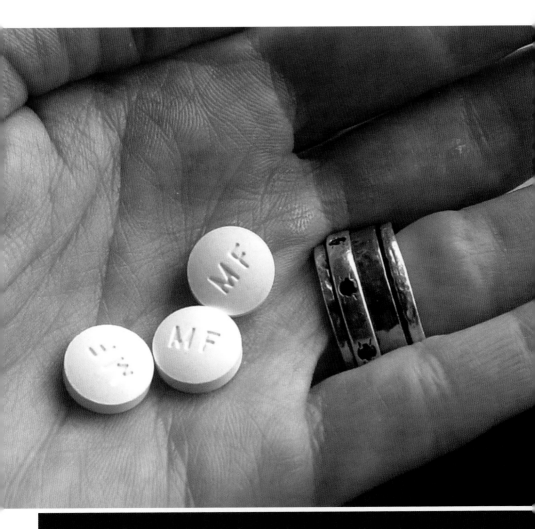

Antiabortion advocates have made the abortion pill (effective until the seventh week of pregnancy) more difficult to use by requiring it to be taken under a doctor's care.

Another form of control that targets women is state-mandated counseling and waiting periods before performing an abortion. In seventeen states, women now must receive counseling before being approved for an abortion. Women are referred for free counseling to "crisis pregnancy centers" (CPCs), which are run by unlicensed antiabortion advocates. It has been reported that they fail to give complete, unbiased information, rather providing feedback that is religiously based and medically inaccurate. By 2013, twenty-six states also required a waiting period (usually twenty-four hours) after counseling before an abortion could be performed. The waiting period in South Dakota and Utah is seventy-two hours. In South Dakota, weekends and holidays are not included, so some women must wait as long as 120 hours (five days).

As of August 2013, twenty-two states required a woman to obtain a medically unnecessary ultrasound image of the fetus before receiving an abortion. An ultrasound adds significantly to the cost of the procedure, and pro-choice advocates feel this requirement is simply meant to discourage women from obtaining abortions. Others state laws limit public funding or insurance coverage for abortions. Forty-six states

Allyson Kirk stands in front of a "crisis pregnancy center" in Manassas, Virginia. Kirk is one of many women who have complained that the clinics give misleading information.

permit private physicians to refuse to perform abortions, and forty-three states allow hospitals to refuse to perform them. Finally, many states require one or both parents to consent to a teen's abortion procedure.

TRAP LAWS: TARGETING ABORTION PROVIDERS

In addition to targeting the women themselves, twenty-seven states so far have TRAP ("targeted regulation of abortion providers") laws. One type of TRAP law strengthens the regulation of abortion clinics as health care providers. In the past, states have required clinics to be licensed and undergo periodic inspections to ensure that they are safe, sanitary, and equipped to handle emergencies. Now, twenty-one states require that abortion providers have admitting privileges or alternatively, transfer arrangements at a local hospital in case of emergencies. These may be impossible to obtain and essentially give hospitals veto power over the clinic's existence. Also, the federal Emergency Medical Treatment and Labor Act of 1986 (EMTALA) makes hospital agreements unnecessary for the patient's health and safety. This act requires hospitals to provide all individuals with emergency treatment. A second type of TRAP law focuses on

THE CASE OF KERMIT GOSNELL

Dr. Kermit Gosnell, a Philadelphia physician, was convicted in May 2013 of first-degree murder for the deaths of three babies born alive at his abortion clinic. While raiding Gosnell's clinic in 2010 to investigate suspected prescription drug trafficking, the FBI discovered forty-seven aborted fetuses stored in clinic freezers. Former clinic employees later testified against Gosnell, stating that he routinely performed abortions after twenty-four weeks (the limit in Pennsylvania) and that he delivered live infants and then killed them by "snipping" their spinal cords. Pro-life advocates see the Gosnell case as proof of the need to ban abortion completely. Pro-choice advocates counter that Gosnell was able to carry out these atrocities because Pennsylvania authorities were negligent and failed to enforce existing regulations. By the time Gosnell was caught, authorities had not inspected state abortion clinics for fifteen years. The scandal led to the firing of two state health officials and stricter rules for Pennsylvania clinics.

changing local zoning and facility requirements. Eighteen states are requiring clinics, even those that provide medication-only (nonsurgical) abortions, to meet all the criteria for surgical centers. These include floor-plan changes (dimensions of procedure rooms, widths of hallways) and outdoor requirements such as number of parking spaces. In Virginia, the average cost for each clinic to comply with required changes ranged from $700,000 to $969,000. These laws force clinics to close because they cannot afford the renovations required.

ARE TRAP LAWS JUSTIFIED?

States that sponsor TRAP laws argue they are protecting women's health and safety. They say abortion is inherently dangerous and requires the same regulations as invasive surgical procedures. Statistics contradict this. According to the Guttmacher Institute, fewer than 0.3 percent of abortion patients have complications requiring hospitalization, and the risk of death from childbirth is fourteen times greater than that from an abortion procedure. The American College of Obstetricians and Gynecologists (ACOG) states that abortion procedures in private physicians' offices are "entirely appropriate," provided the physician is equipped to handle emergencies. The Supreme Court, in *Akron v. Akron Center for Reproductive Health* (1983), ruled that there was no justification for requiring second-trimester abortions to be carried out in a hospital, based on protecting women's health and safety.

Some state officials are open about the reasons for TRAP laws and other abortion restrictions.

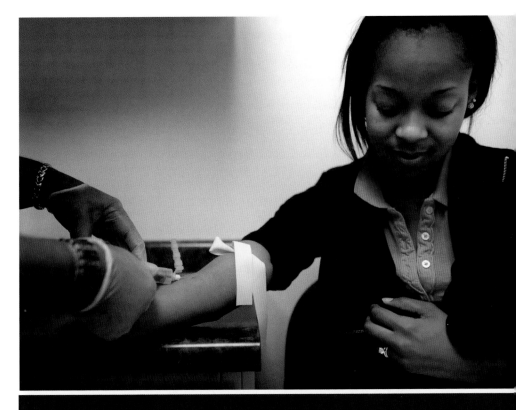

Minah Khan, twenty-four, receives all of her reproductive health care from a Planned Parenthood clinic. This includes blood tests for preventive care.

When Republican governor Phil Bryant signed Mississippi's 2012 TRAP bill into law, he said, "Today you see the first step in a movement to do what we campaigned on...to try to end abortion in Mississippi." This law resulted in closing the state's last abortion clinic in 2013.

One factor seldom considered when states close abortion clinics is that these clinics provide more than abortions. Only 3 percent of Planned Parenthood's services are abortion services. Rather, they provide comprehensive reproductive health services, including Pap smears, cancer screenings, tests for sexually trans-mitted diseases, contraceptive information and access, and prenatal care. Closing these clinics thus denies many poor women access not only to abortion, but also to all basic reproductive health care.

Evidence indicates that, since the *Roe v. Wade* and *Doe v. Bolton* decisions in 1973, abortion rights in the United States have eroded. Although the Supreme Court has not overturned the decision, it has made several decisions weakening it. But the greatest ero-sion has come from the barrage of state laws that have increasingly restricted the ability of women to access abortion, doctors to perform it, and clinics to remain open to provide the service.

CHAPTER SIX

ABORTION UNDER SIEGE: THE FUTURE OF REPRODUCTIVE RIGHTS

In 2009, gynecologist Dr. George Tiller was murdered in his Wichita, Kansas, church by an antiabortion extremist. Tiller's clinic closed and since then, women in western Kansas needing abortion services have had to travel three hours or more to clinics in Kansas City or Oklahoma. Julie Burkhart, who had worked with Dr. Tiller, vowed to open a new clinic. She founded the Trust Women Foundation, which purchased Dr. Tiller's old clinic in 2012. South Winds Women's Center opened in April 2013. The new center provides complete gynecological care, including abortions through fourteen weeks. It refers to other medical facilities those women needing later-term abortions.

Antiabortion activists from Operation Rescue fought the center's opening. They tried to get the site rezoned and filed bogus complaints with building inspectors and fire

Julie Burkhart, executive director of the South Winds Women's Center in Wichita, Kansas, stands before a photo of Dr. George Tiller, who was murdered by an antiabortion extremist in 2009.

departments. They picketed Burkhart's home with threatening signs, causing her to seek a protection order and tighten security both at home and at the clinic. Two of the center's three doctors, who have tried to remain anonymous for safety reasons, fly in from out of state. One Illinois doctor was "outed" by Operation Rescue's Troy Newman, who described her as the new owner of the South Winds Women's Center. Since the center opened in Wichita, antiabortion groups have led monthly protests in front of her family practice clinic near Chicago.

Opening the Wichita clinic has been a struggle. Burkhart fears for her own safety and that of clinic employees, but she remains committed. "Why," she says, "just because we live in Kansas...should women be faced with more hardship? Why should it just be women on the coast ... that have access to abortion care?"

THE ABORTION FIGHT TODAY

This story illustrates the extremes of the abortion controversy in the second decade of the twenty-first century. Lines are drawn, and both sides are resolute. Both picket, lobby, and join organizations. Pro-life groups try to change abortion laws; when laws are changed, pro-choice groups file lawsuits trying to overturn them. The fringes of the antiabortion side resort to threats and even violence. Scott Roeder, Dr. Tiller's murderer, admitted that he shot Tiller because "pre-born children were in imminent danger." These two groups do not represent a mere difference of opinion; they have a difference of beliefs so strong that compromise seems impossible.

Presently, the antiabortion side of the controversy seems to be strongest. Many states are passing laws that restrict abortion access. Abortion-rights activists are suing, but with limited success. In Kansas, Planned Parenthood sued to block a requirement to provide women with medically inaccurate information, but a U.S. district judge refused the request. In July 2013, North Carolina passed antiabortion legislation by attaching it to bills on other subjects. The Senate tacked abortion restrictions onto a bill banning Sharia law (the religious law of Islam). The House tweaked the bill slightly

BUCKING THE TREND

New York and Washington State have tried—so far, unsuccessfully—to pass laws that would increase abortion access. In New York, Governor Andrew Cuomo's Women's Equality Agenda included a measure to decriminalize abortion after twenty-four weeks when the woman's health (instead of her life only) was in danger. Senate Democratic leaders removed this measure from the bill. Although they support abortion rights, they lacked enough Senate votes to pass the bill.

In Washington State, a bill requiring all insurance providers to cover abortion if they cover prenatal care also failed to pass in the Senate. Abortion rights activists supported the bill, fearing coverage might decrease when the Affordable Care Act took effect. Planned Parenthood Great Northwest stated, "[T]his bill would ensure that women—not politicians, nor bosses—make their own private medical decisions." Critics of the bill said it was unnecessary because health insurers in Washington already provide for abortion coverage.

and attached it to a motorcycle safety bill. The North Carolina governor says the new bill will not limit access to abortion. However, opponents say the cost of meeting new design standards required by the bill will shut down most of the state's clinics.

THE MODERATE MIDDLE

Those on the "pro-life" side of the issue want to ban abortion entirely. Those on the "pro-choice" side support abortion on demand throughout pregnancy. Most people are somewhere in the middle. They do not like abortion and they do not prefer it as a method of birth control—but they also accept that, under certain circumstances, it is necessary. Therefore, it should be safe and legally available. Many people favor abortion access early in pregnancy (before viability) but want it regulated later (after viability).

The Gallup organization has conducted polls on attitudes toward abortion since 1975. In 1978, 22 percent of responders thought abortion should be legal under any circumstances, 19 percent thought it should never be legal, and 55 percent thought it should be legal only under certain circumstances. In 2013, the value for "always legal" was 26 percent, for "always illegal" was 22 percent, and "legal under certain circumstances" was 52 percent. Thus, despite minor variations from year to year, slightly more than half of those surveyed continue to think abortion should be regulated but legal under some circumstances.

JUDICIAL OBJECTIONS TO *ROE V. WADE*

Several legal scholars and Supreme Court justices favor abortion rights but disagree with the way the United States has handled the issue. Justice Ruth Bader Ginsburg has criticized *Roe* because it did not consider women's rights, but only a doctor's freedom to practice. She stated, "Also in the balance is a woman's autonomous charge of her full life's course, her ability to stand in relation to men, society and to stay as an independent, self-sustaining

A star at Harvard Law School, Ruth Bader Ginsburg was denied jobs because she was female. As a Supreme Court Justice, she has been a strong advocate for women's rights.

equal citizen." Ginsburg felt abortion rights should have been handled legislatively, as part of the women's movement. She was not alone.

Legal scholars, including Professors John Hart Ely and Laurence Tribe, have questioned the ruling's constitutionality. These scholars felt the decision could not be inferred from the language of the Constitution and that the Court was therefore legislating, rather than interpreting, the Constitution. Richard Gregory Morgan states: "The stark inadequacy of the Court's attempt to justify its conclusions...suggests to some scholars that the Court, finding no justification at all in the Constitution, unabashedly usurped the legislative function." Antiabortion groups use these and similar objections to *Roe v. Wade*'s constitutionality to discredit the decision. Other scholars, including Jeffrey Rosen and Michael Kinsley, suggest that legislating the right to abortion, rather than deciding it judicially, would have provided a much stronger basis for public support. The British journal the *Economist* sees the Supreme Court decision as "calculated to stir up controversy," pointing out that it gave abortion opponents no say in the decision and left supporters at the mercy of the changing balance of power on the Supreme Court.

WHO OBTAINS ABORTIONS AND WHY?

Statistics from the Guttmacher Institute show that 18 percent of women obtaining abortions are teenagers and 57 percent are in their twenties. Non-Hispanic white women account for 36 percent of abortions, non-Hispanic black women for 30 percent, and Hispanic women for 25 percent. Approximately 61 percent of women obtaining abortions already have one or more children. Many are extremely poor—42 percent have incomes less than 100 percent of the federal poverty level (which, in 2013, was $10,830 for a single woman with no children). When asked their reasons for seeking an abortion, three-fourths cite responsibility for other people, inability to afford a child, or inability to care for a child and meet current responsibilities (work, school, or care of other dependents). Half do not want to be single parents or are having problems with partners.

These statistics indicate that the people most affected by changes in abortion laws are poor women, many of them single and from minority groups. Many of these women (54 percent) used contraception, but either the contraception failed or they used it incorrectly. The other 46 percent did not use contraceptives—33 percent thought they had little risk of pregnancy, 32 percent were concerned about safety of contraceptive methods, 26 percent had unexpected sex, and 1 percent were raped. Eight percent of women seeking abortions have never used birth control. Most of these women are poor, young, less well-educated, and black or Hispanic. Teenage girls are at particular risk. Parental notification or consent laws often backfire. Teens may fear telling their parents about a pregnancy because of abuse, incest, and similar reasons. Instead, they seek unsafe, illegal abortions.

Pro-life activists advocate abstinence over contraception. If a woman has an unwanted pregnancy, they advocate adoption over abortion. Pro-choice advocates feel that all women should have access to

A mobile health clinic in Garland, Texas, provides medical assistance for teenage mothers, such as Evelyn Flores, shown here in 2006 with her month-old daughter.

contraceptive education and materials and complete information about their options (including abortion) in case of pregnancy. They would prefer decreases in abortion, but they think access to and education about contraception and abortion are more likely to accomplish this than restrictive laws.

CURRENT TRENDS IN ATTITUDE

Judicial objections, combined with increasingly strict interpretations of Court decisions by many states, suggest that abortion rights in the United States might be overturned. However, abortion rights, in some form, have become an integral part of American law and life. After forty years, many women take the availability of abortion for granted. Thus, attempts to eliminate this right will likely meet with resistance.

Wendy Davis's filibuster in the Texas legislature in June 2013, which drew attention to attempts to restrict abortion rights and energized activists, is one example. With regard to the Texas restrictions, Davis said after her filibuster, "It's big government intruding in private lives in Texas, and Texas values don't cotton to that very well." Some thought the 2013 conviction of Philadelphia abortionist Kermit Gosnell would cause people to demand an end to abortion. Indeed, pro-life groups are using the case as evidence for banning abortion. But pro-choice groups counter that proper enforcement of existing laws would have prevented Gosnell's criminal activities. A Gallup poll on the matter indicated that the Gosnell case had not shifted Americans' views on abortion.

Individual attitudes often change little because abortion is such an emotional and polarizing issue. Laws change more readily, and occasionally challenges to state laws reach the Supreme Court. Because the composition of the Court changes periodically, the law may be overturned at some point (although there is strong precedent for keeping it). In short, despite today's trends, it is impossible to predict tomorrow's changes. The only thing that seems certain is that abortion will continue to be a polarizing issue that affects not only our legal and political landscapes, but also people's lives.

GLOSSARY

abortifacient An agent (usually a drug) that induces an abortion.

abortion The termination (usually intentional) of a human pregnancy; also, the spontaneous expulsion of an embryo during the first twelve weeks of pregnancy.

burden of proof The duty of proving a charge disputed in court.

conception The moment when the chromosomes of an egg and sperm combine to form a unique biological entity; also called fertilization.

contraception Birth control; use of devices, agents, or drugs to prevent pregnancy before it occurs.

embryo An unborn entity in the first eight weeks of pregnancy, before organs are fully developed.

eugenics A belief that the human species can be genetically improved by selective breeding or sterilization.

fetus An unborn entity from eight weeks of pregnancy until birth.

filibuster Use of obstructionist tactics, usually prolonged speech-making, to delay or prevent a vote or to force a decision against the will of the majority.

genocide Deliberate killing of a large group of people of the same race, ethnic group, religion, or nation.

gynecology The branch of medicine dealing with health care and diseases of women, particularly the female reproductive system.

implantation Attachment of the tiny embryo to the uterine wall; occurs several days after conception.

miscarriage The accidental death of an unborn child.

obstetrics The branch of medicine and surgery dealing with childbirth and care of women giving birth.

partial-birth abortion Abortion during the second trimester of pregnancy, usually twenty to twenty-four weeks; done by a process called dilation and extraction (D&X); now illegal.

plaintiff A person who brings a suit in a court of law; accuser or complaining party.

precedent A court case cited as an example to help decide future cases.

prima facie Legally sufficient; a legal term meaning "accepted as correct until proven otherwise."

quickening An older term meaning the first movement of the fetus, which occurs at about the fourth month of pregnancy.

telemedicine Providing medical care and information electronically, for example, via e-mail, text, or remote contact (such as Skype).

viable In abortion law, capable of meaningful life outside a woman's uterus (noun: viability).

FOR MORE INFORMATION

Abortion Rights Coalition of Canada (ARCC)
P.O. Box 2663, Station Main
Vancouver, BC V6B 3W3
Canada
(888) 642-2725
E-mail: info@arcc-cdac.ca
Web site: http://www.arcc-cdac.ca
This pro-choice volunteer organization works
toward reproductive freedom for all women,
including the right to safe, accessible abortion.

Americans United for Life (AUL)
655 15th Street NW, Suite 410
Washington, DC 20005
(202) 289-1478
E-mail: info@aul.org
Web site: http://www.aul.org
AUL is a nonprofit, public-interest law and policy
organization working for the pro-life movement
for the "legal protection for human life from
conception to natural death." It has worked on
every abortion-related case before the U.S.
Supreme Court since *Roe v. Wade.*

Canadian Federation for Sexual Health
2197 Riverside Drive, Suite 403

Ottawa, ON K1H 7X3
Canada
(613) 241-4474
E-mail: admin@cfsh.ca
Web site: http://www.cfsh.ca
The Canadian Federation for Sexual Health is a
    national, nongovernmental, volunteer organiza-
    tion dedicated to sexual and reproductive health
    and rights and is a member of the International
    Planned Parenthood Federation. It supports
    birth planning by assuring adequate education
    and services for all Canadians.

Center for Reproductive Rights
120 Wall Street
New York, NY 10005
(917) 637-3600
Web site: http://reproductiverights.org
This nonprofit legal and policy advocacy organiza-
    tion promotes women's reproductive rights
    through programs that engage in litigation, pol-
    icy analysis, legal research, and public education.
    It produces reports, organizing packets, and edu-
    cational materials.

Family Research Council
801 G Street NW

Washington, DC 20001

(800) 225-4008

Web site: http://www.frc.org

The Family Research Council is a conservative
Christian think tank dedicated to promoting
"traditional family values." It promotes absti-
nence-only programs and works against
reproductive freedom, sex education, and equal
rights for gays and lesbians.

Guttmacher Institute

125 Maiden Lane, 7th floor

New York, NY 10038

(212) 248-1111

1301 Connecticut Avenue NW, Suite 700

Washington, DC 20036

(202) 296-4012

Web site: http://www.guttmacher.org

This nonprofit research and policy center studies
and provides information and statistics on
reproductive health, particularly abortion and
contraception.

Ipas

P.O. Box 9990

Chapel Hill, NC 27515

(800) 334-8446

Web site: http://www.ipas.org/en.aspx

This global, nongovernmental organization of public health professionals works to end deaths and
medical problems related to unsafe abortion.
They work around the world to provide safe
abortion care, plus counseling and contraception
to prevent future unintended pregnancies.

National Abortion and Reproductive Rights Action
League (NARAL)

1156 15th Street NW, Suite 700

Washington, DC 20005

(202) 973-3000

E-mail: CAN@ProChoiceAmerica.org

Web site: http://www.prochoiceamerica.org

NARAL uses the political process to guarantee every
woman the right to make personal decisions
regarding the full range of reproductive choices,
including legal abortion. It produces publications
including congressional voting records and state-
by-state analysis of reproductive rights legislation.

National Right to Life Committee

512 10th Street NW

Washington, DC 20004

(202) 626-8800

E-mail: NRLC@nrlc.org

Web site: http://www.nrlc.org

This national pro-life organization has affiliates in all fifty states and works to ban abortion in the United States. It consists of three separate entities: the National Right to Life Committee, the National Right to Life Educational Trust Fund, and the National Right to Life Political Action Committee.

Operation Rescue

P.O. Box 782888

Wichita, KS 67278

(316) 683-6790

E-mail: info.operationrescue@gmail.com

Web site: http://www.operationrescue.org

Operation Rescue is a Christian pro-life activist organization whose major goal is to reduce abortion access in the United States, primarily by actively working to close abortion clinics.

Planned Parenthood Federation of America (PPFA)

434 West 33rd Street

New York, NY 10001

(212) 541-7800

E-mail: communications@ppfa.org

Web site: http://www.plannedparenthood.org

PPFA provides comprehensive reproductive health care services, while preserving and protecting the privacy and rights of individuals. It advocates policies that guarantee these rights and services, provides educational programs, and promotes research on reproductive health care.

WEB SITES

Due to the changing nature of Internet links, Rosen Publishing has developed an online list of Web sites related to the subject of this book. This site is updated regularly. Please use this link to access the list:

http://www.rosenlinks.com/UUSC/Abor

FOR FURTHER READING

Acred, Cara. *The Abortion Debate: 231 (Issues Today*, Vol. 231). Cambridge, England: Independence Educational Publishers; Amazon Digital Services Inc., Kindle edition, 2012.

Berlatsky, Noah. *Abortion* (Global Viewpoints). Farmington Hills, MI: Greenhaven Press, 2010.

Berne, Emma Carlson. *Abortion* (Introducing Issues with Opposing Viewpoints). Farmington Hills, MI: Greenhaven Press, 2007.

Bowling, Dusti. *The Day We Met*. Tower.com, Inc.: Ketina Publishing House, Kindle edition, 2011.

Calkin, Abigail B. *The Carolyne Letters: A Story of Birth, Abortion, and Adoption*. Salt Lake City, UT: Familius, 2013.

Englander, Anrenee, ed. *Dear Diary, I'm Pregnant: Ten Real Life Stories*. Toronto, ON, Canada: Annick Press, Amazon Digital Services, Inc., Kindle edition, 2010.

Farrell, Courtney. *The Abortion Debate* (Essential Viewpoints). Edina, MN: ABDO Publishing, 2008.

Friedman, Lauri S. *Abortion* (Compact Research). San Diego, CA: ReferencePoint Press, 2008.

Greenhaven Press eds. *Abortion* (Opposing Viewpoints). Farmington Hills, MI: Greenhaven Press, 2013.

Haugen, David M. *Abortion* (Opposing Viewpoints). Farmington Hills, MI: Greenhaven Press, 2010.

Higgins, Melissa. *Roe v. Wade: Abortion and a Woman's Right to Privacy* (Landmark Supreme Court Cases). Edina, MN: ABDO Publishing Company, 2012.

Knapp, Lynette. *The Abortion Controversy* (Current Controversies). Farmington Hills, MI: Greenhaven Press, 2007.

Lanier, Wendy. *Abortion* (Hot Topics). San Diego, CA: Lucent Books. 2009.

Leverich, Jean, ed. *Abortion* (Issues on Trial). Farmington Hills, MI: Greenhaven Press, 2010.

Marcovitz, Hal. *Abortion* (Gallup Major Trends and Events). Broomall, PA: Mason Crest, 2007.

Merino, No'l, ed. *Abortion* (Opposing Viewpoints). Farmington Hills, MI: Greenhaven Press, 2012.

Roleff, Tamara, ed. *Are Abortion Rights Threatened?* (At Issue Series). Farmington Hills, MI: Greenhaven Press, 2013.

Shusterman, Neal. *Unwind* (Unwind Dystology). New York, NY: Simon & Schuster Books for Young Readers, 2009.

BIBLIOGRAPHY

Beckwith, Francis J. *Defending Life: A Moral and Legal Case Against Abortion Choice.* New York, NY: Cambridge University Press, 2007.

Boonstra, Heather. "Medication Abortion Restrictions Burden Women and Providers—and Threaten U.S. Trend Toward Very Early Abortions." *Guttmacher Policy Review*, Vol. 16, No. 1., Winter 2013. Retrieved August 10, 2013.

Bullington, Jonathan. "Justice Ginsburg: *Roe v. Wade* Not 'Woman-Centered.'" *Chicago Tribune*, May 11, 2013. Retrieved August 9, 2013 (http://articles .chicagotribune.com/2013-05-11/news/chi-justice -ginsburg-roe-v-wade-not-womancentered-20130511 _1_roe-v-abortion-related-cases-wade-case).

Center for Reproductive Rights. "U.S. Supreme Court Case Summaries: Privacy Law 1891–Present." 1992–2013. Retrieved July 17, 2013 (http://repro-ductiverights.org/en/document/ us-supreme-court-case-summaries-privacy-law- 1891-present).

Economist Special Report. "Abortion in America. The War That Never Ends." *Economist*, January 16, 2003. Retrieved August 8, 2013 (http://www.econ-omist.com/node/1534731).

Ely, John Hart. "The Wages of Crying Wolf: A Comment on *Roe v. Wade*." Yale Law School Legal Scholarship

Repository, January 1, 1973. Retrieved August 9, 2013 (http://digitalcommons.law.yale.edu/cgi/viewcontent.cgi?article=5116&context=fss_papers).

Gold, Rachel Benson, and Elizabeth Nash. "TRAP Laws Gain Political Traction While Abortion Clinics—and the Women They Serve—Pay the Price." *Guttmacher Policy Review*, Vol. 16, No. 2. Spring 2013. Retrieved August 5, 2013 (http://www.guttmacher.org/pubs/gpr/16/2/gpr160207.html).

Greenhouse, Linda, and Reva B. Siegel. *Before Roe v. Wade: Voices That Shaped the Abortion Debate Before the Supreme Court's Ruling.* New York, NY: Kaplan Publishing, 2010.

Guttmacher Institute. "An Overview of Abortion Laws." August 1, 2013. Retrieved August 4, 2013 (http://www.guttmacher.org/statecenter/spibs/spib_OAL.pdf).

Hull, N. E. H., and Peter Charles Hoffer. *Roe v. Wade: The Abortion Rights Controversy in American History.* 2nd ed., revised and expanded. Lawrence, KS: University Press of Kansas, 2010.

McBride, Alex. "Supreme Court History: *Roe v. Wade* (1973)." PBS: The Supreme Court, December 2006. Retrieved July 17, 2013 (http://www.pbs.org/wnet/supremecourt/rights/landmark_roe.html).

Morgan, Richard Gregory. "*Roe v. Wade* and the
Lesson of the Pre-*Roe* Case Law." *Michigan Law
Review* 77 (1979): 1,724–48, excerpted in: "Legal
Scholars" (http://old.usccb.org/prolife/issues/abor-
tion/roevwade/LegalSchol.pdf).

National Abortion Federation. "History of Abortion."
2010. Retrieved July 2, 2013 (http://www.prochoice
.org/about_abortion/history_abortion.html).

On the Issues. "Ruth Bader Ginsburg on Abortion."
Senate Nomination Hearing, Excerpts in *New
York Times*, July 22, 1993. Retrieved August 9,
2013 (http://www.ontheissues.org/Court/Ruth_
Bader_Ginsburg_Abortion.htm).

Oyez.org. "*Griswold v. Connecticut*." IIT Chicago-
Kent College of Law, U.S. Supreme Court Media.
2005–2011. Retrieved July 15, 2013 (http://www
.oyez.org/cases/1960-1969/1964/1964_496).

PBS Online. "People and Events: Anthony Comstock's
'Chastity' Laws." *The Pill*, 1999–2001. Retrieved
July 3, 2013 (http://www.pbs.org/wgbh/amex/pill/
peopleevents/e_comstock.html).

Pew Forum on Religion & Public Life. "A History of
Key Abortion Rulings of the U.S. Supreme Court."
Pew Research Center, January 16, 2013. Retrieved
July 26, 2013 (http://www.pewforum.org/
Abortion/A-History-of-Key-Abortion-Rulings
-of-the-US-Supreme-Court.aspx).

Pollitt, Katha. "Abortion in American History."
    Atlantic Monthly, Vol. 279, No. 5, pp. 111–115.
    May 1997 (http://www.theatlantic.com/past/docs/
    issues/97may/abortion.htm).

Reagan, Leslie. *When Abortion Was a Crime:
    Women, Medicine, and Law in the United States,
    1867–1973*. Berkeley, CA: University of
    California Press, 1997.

Rose, Melody. *Safe, Legal, and Unavailable? Abortion
    Politics in the United States*. Washington, DC: CQ
    Press, 2007.

Rosen, Jeffrey. "Worst Choice: Why We'd Be Better Off
    Without *Roe*." *New Republic*, February 19, 2003.
    Retrieved August 9, 2013 (http://brothersjuddblog
    .com/archives/2003/02/give_the_people_a_choice
    _via_r.html).

Siegel, Neil S., and Reva B. Siegel. "Equality
    Arguments for Abortion Rights." *UCLA Law
    Review* 60 Disc. 160, 2013. Retrieved July 22,
    2013 (http://www.uclalawreview.org/?p=4186).

INDEX

ABOUT THE AUTHOR

Carol Hand has a Ph.D. in zoology. She has taught college biology (including human anatomy and physiology), written assessments and curricula for middle and high school, and authored a number of young-adult books on science and social studies. She has followed and studied the abortion debate, with a special interest in its biological and social perspectives.

PHOTO CREDITS

Cover, p. 87 McClatchy-Tribune/Getty Images; p. 3 spirit of america/Shutterstock.com; pp. 4, 40, 55, 82–83, 90–91 © AP Images; pp. 7, 22, 37, 51, 64, 81 Mikhail Kolesnikov/Shutterstock.com; p. 7 (inset) Karen Bleier/AFP/Getty Images; p. 10 © Wagstaff Collection/Mary Evans/The Image Works; p. 12 Library of Congress Prints and Photographs Division; pp. 14–15 Science & Society Picture Library/Getty Images; p. 18 Lynn Johnson/National Geographic Image Collection/Getty Images; pp. 23, 24–25 MPI/Archive Photos/Getty Images; pp. 30–31 Cynthia Johnson/Time & Life Pictures/Getty Images; p. 32 National Geographic/SuperStock; p. 36 Win McNamee/Getty Images; p. 44 Hulton Archive/Getty Images; p. 45 New York Daily News Archive/Getty Images; p. 47 Fuse/Getty Images; p. 49 Kristian Sekulic/E+/Getty Images; pp. 51 (inset), 79 The Washington Post/Getty Images; p. 53 Greg Gibson/AFP/Getty Images; p. 57 Clouds Hill Imaging Ltd/Science Photo Library/Getty Images; p. 69 Jonathan Ernst/Getty Images; p. 71 Guttmacher Institute, New York. "2012 Saw Second-Highest Number of Abortion Restrictions Ever." Guttmacher.org. www.guttmacher.org/media/inthenews/2013/01/02/ (accessed October 31, 2013); pp. 72–73 Bill Greenblatt/Hulton Archive/Getty Images; pp. 74–75 Chicago Tribune/McClatchy-Tribune/Getty Images; cover and interior design elements: design36/Shutterstock.com, Eky Studio/Shutterstock.com, Flame of life/Shutterstock.com, Brandon Bourdages/Shutterstock.com; back cover (Constitution detail) J. Helgason/Shutterstock.com.

Designer: Michael Moy; Editor: Hope Laurie Killcoyne; Photo Researcher: Cindy Reiman